Crafts, crafts, more crafts!

101 great ideas for youth and children's clubs

DayOne

© Day One Publications 2010

First printed 2010

ISBN 978-1-84625-228-0

British Library Cataloguing in Publication Data available

Published by Day One Publications

Ryelands Road, Leominster, England, HR6 8NZ

Telephone 01568 613 740   FAX 01568 611 473

email—sales@dayone.co.uk

web site—www.dayone.co.uk

North American e-mail—usasales@dayone.co.uk

North American web site—www.dayonebookstore.com

Printed by Thomson Litho, East Kilbride, Scotland

Dedication

For my sisters Esther, Abigail and
Miriam, and my niece Naomi

For the Missionary Kids of UFM
on whom I have tested many of my
ideas over the years

Endorsements

At last, a book filled with practical ideas for craft activities that relate to children's ministry and that don't cost the earth or require proximity to a specialist craft shop. What sets this book apart is the simplicity of the ideas and the use of easily accessible materials, many being recycled household objects.

These are the sort of ideas that can be taken as they are or adapted to suit the age of the audience, and the Bible verse or topic being taught.

Having seen Tirzah in action with my own children at a UFM family conference and witnessed the enjoyment they got out of making some of these crafts, I am delighted to see this book in print.

Rosalind Brown, missionary with UFM Worldwide, children's worker and mother of five

As someone who has spent years trying to do crafts for young people, and hunting about for ideas that work, a book like this is invaluable. All the ideas in one place and simply explained saves me hours of scratching my head and pestering others for ideas. Well done!

Liz Dakin, youth worker for 25 years at Wem Baptist Church

Contents

A Quick Guide to Glue

I haven't always specified which glue to use, so here is a quick guide to which glue to use when!

PVA
Most versatile of the 'glue family' —it is used for paper, card, fabrics, wood, plaster etc. It is a milky white colour in the bottle but dries clear.

Super Glue
Should only be used under supervision as it bonds instantly to whatever it touches; generally used for china, metals etc.

All Purpose
Strong and clear—it can be used for most crafts.

Glitter Glue
Used for decorative purposes—it gives a 3D effect.

Glue Sticks
Non-messy, stops paper wrinkling (PVA can have that effect as it is water based) great for kids, useful for paper crafts, but not always very strong.

Sticky Fixers
Great for card making, non-messy— it comes in a variety of depths and gives a great raised effect.

There are many more types of glue but these are the ones generally used in crafts.

Note

All leaders should check the child protection and health and safety policies of their church or organization before making these crafts and ensure that they follow the requirements laid out in them.

Old Testament

1 Creation: Metallic stars and moon

What you need

Tinfoil trays
Sharp scissors
Hole punch
Ribbon

Bible link

Genesis 1–2

How to make it

1. Cut out stars and moon shapes from the tinfoil trays. Be careful as the edges may be sharp.

2. Punch a hole in the shape and thread some ribbon through. Tie a knot in the ribbon to hang the shapes up.

3. Don't worry if the trays have small holes in them as this creates a nice effect when the sun shines on them.

2 Noah 1: Tissue paper rainbow

What you need

A4 card
Pen
Tissue paper (red, orange, yellow,
    green, blue, indigo and violet)
Glue

Bible link

'I have set my rainbow in the clouds,
and it will be the sign of the covenant
between me and the earth.'
                        Genesis 9:13

How to make it

1. Draw a rainbow on the card,
   marking separate lines for each
   colour.

2. Put glue on the first stripe.

3. Screw up the red tissue paper into
   small balls and stick them on to the
   card, covering the whole stripe.

4. Repeat Steps 2 and 3 for each colour.

3 Noah 2: Footprint rainbow

What you need

Large sheet of blue card
Paint (red, orange, yellow, green, blue, indigo and violet)
White paper

Bible link

'I have set my rainbow in the clouds, and it will be the sign of the covenant between me and the earth.'

Genesis 9:13

How to make it

1. Make a footprint on a sheet of white paper in each colour of paint.

2. When the footprints have dried cut them out and glue them onto the blue card in the shape of a rainbow.

3. Write an appropriate memory verse in the footprints.

4 Tower of Babel: Flag coaster

What you need

Card squares (approximately 10cm x 10cm)
Colouring pens
Laminate pouches
Laminator
Book of flags of the world

Bible link

'That is why it was called Babel—because there the LORD confused the language of the whole world. From there the LORD scattered them over the face of the whole earth.'

Genesis 11:9

How to make it

1. Get each child to draw and colour a flag of their choice on the card square. If time, they could make several.

2. Laminate the card squares.

5 Joseph 1: Joseph's coat

What you need

Very large sheet of card
Lots of scraps of material
Glue
Colouring pens

Bible link

'Now Israel loved Joseph more than any of his other sons, because he had been born to him in his old age; and he made a richly ornamented robe for him.'

Genesis 37:3

How to make it

1. This is a group activity

2. Draw an outline of a man on the card and then cut it out. Make it as large as you can.

3. Cover the body in PVA glue.

4. Cover the body in the scraps of material.

5. Colour in the face, hands and feet and you have a large Joseph!

6 Joseph 2: Pyramids

What you need

Card
PVA glue
Sand
Brown paint

Bible link

The Israelites in Egypt

Exodus 1–18

How to make it

1. Cut out four identical triangles (leaving flaps on the side for sticking).

2. Glue all four triangles together.

3. Cut a square the size of the base and glue it into place.

4. Paint the pyramid brown and leave it to dry.

5. Cover it in a light layer of PVA glue.

6. Lightly shake sand over the pyramid and leave it to dry.

7 Moses: Baby Moses in the bulrushes

What you need

An egg carton (which holds 6 eggs)
Sharp scissors
Brown paint
Scraps of cloth
Instructions for making people

Bible link

'But when she could hide [Moses] no longer, she got a papyrus basket for him and coated it with tar and pitch. Then she placed the child in it and put it among the reeds along the bank of the Nile.'

Exodus 2:3

How to make it

1. Holding the egg box lengthways cut about a third off the top section.

2. Pain brown all over, inside and out, then leave to dry.

3. Using one of the patterns found in the 'people' section make a baby Moses.

4. Place Moses in the basket and cover with the cloth.

5. Close the lid.

8 Moses: Burning bush

What you need

Branch with no leaves
Red and gold tissue paper
Scissors
Sticky tape

Bible link

'There the angel of the LORD
appeared to him in flames of fire from
within a bush. Moses saw that
though the bush was on fire it did not
burn up.'

Exodus 3:2

How to make it

1. Cut out lots of leaves from the tissue paper.

2. Tape the leaves all over the branch.

9 Ten plagues: Plagues wheel

What you need

2 pieces of card
Paper fasteners
Scissors
Colouring pens

Bible link

Exodus 7–12

How to make it

1. Cut out two circles of card the same size.

2. Divide one piece into ten equal size sections.

3. Draw a picture of each plague in each section.

4. On the second piece of card cut out a section the same size and shape as one section.

5. Place the second piece of card over the first and secure with paper fastener

6. Turn the wheel to see each of the plagues in turn.

10 Ten commandments: Parchment

What you need

Thick white paper
Cold tea or coffee
Hair dryer
Thin permanent marker pen
Baking tray
Ribbon

Bible link

Exodus 20:1–21

How to make it

1. Take the white paper and rip around the edges. (Do not use scissors or make it too neat.)

2. Crumple the paper as tight as possible into a ball.

3. Flatten the paper and place it on a baking tray.

4. Pour the tea or coffee over both sides making sure it's totally covered.

5. Pour off any excess tea or coffee.

6. Dry the paper with the hairdryer while it is still on the baking tray.

7. When it is completely dry write the ten commandments on the paper.

8. Roll into a scroll and secure with ribbon.

11 David and Goliath 1: Door stop

What you need

Large smooth stone
Acrylic paint
PVA glue
Water

Bible link

1 Samuel 17

How to make it

1. Find a large smooth stone. (You can buy these at a garden centre.)

2. Decorate with acrylic paint.

3. Paint a suitable memory verse on or a picture of David and Goliath.

4. To varnish mix PVA glue and water together.

12 David and Goliath 2: David's shepherd's pouch

What you need

Brown felt
Large metal darning needle
Brown embroidery thread

Bible link

'Then [David] took his staff in his hand, chose five smooth stones from the stream, put them in the pouch of his shepherd's bag and, with his sling in his hand, approached the Philistine.'

1 Samuel 17:40

How to make it

1. Cut the brown felt into a circle.

2. Using the embroidery thread at full thickness sew loosely around the edge of the circle.

3. Pull the ends together to make a small pouch.

4. Put five small stones inside.

Note:
A fun alternative is to use chocolate mini eggs.

13 David and Jonathan 1: Framed friend

What you need

Picture of your friend
Cardboard
Decorating materials
Glue
String

Bible link

1 Samuel 18:1–4

How to make it

1. Cut the card into four strips to make a frame. Measure the picture to get the correct lengths.

2. Fix the card strips to the edges of the picture.

3. Decorate the frame.

4. Fix a loop of string on the back of the picture.

14 David and Jonathan 2: Friendship bracelet

What you need

Embroidery threads (at least three
  different colours)
Sticky tape

Bible link

'After David had finished talking with
Saul, Jonathan became one in spirit
with David, and he loved him as
himself.'

1 Samuel 18:1

How to make it

1. Choose three different colours of
   thread.

2. Keep the embroidery thread at full
   thickness.

3. Cut the thread slightly longer than
   the circumference of the wrist of
   recipient.

4. Tie the three ends together.

5. Tape the knot to the table. This
   keeps the threads steady.

6. Plait the threads to the end, making
   sure that you keep it nice and tight.

7. Tie off the end of the plait and tie the
   two ends together to make a bracelet.

15 Jonah: Egg box boat

What you need

Egg carton lid
Material scraps
Straw
Sticky tape
Adhesive putty
Brown paint

Bible link

'But Jonah ran away from the LORD and headed for Tarshish. He went down to Joppa, where he found a ship bound for that port. After paying the fare, he went aboard and sailed for Tarshish to flee from the LORD.'

Jonah 1:3

How to make it

1. Paint the egg carton lid inside and out, then leave to dry.

2. Cut a sail from the material and attach it to the straw using sticky tape.

3. Fix the straw inside the lid using adhesive putty.

16 Isaiah: Simple origami tulip

What you need

2 green straws
Square of red paper
Sticky tape

Bible link

'The grass withers and the flowers fall, but the word of our God stands for ever.'

Isaiah 40:8

How to make it

1. Fold the square into a triangle. Have the point facing away from you.

2. Take the bottom left hand corner and fold up to the middle point.

3. Repeat with the bottom right hand corner.

4. Cut one straw in half and stick the halves onto the full length one to make the stem.

5. Stick the straw onto the tulip head.

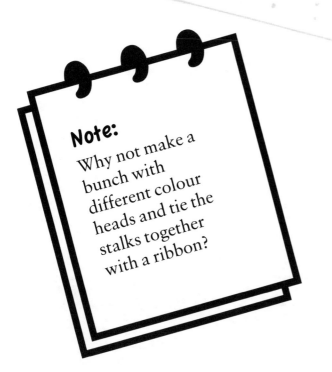

Note:
Why not make a bunch with different colour heads and tie the stalks together with a ribbon?

17 Joshua and Jericho: Paper trumpets

What you need

Coloured paper
Party blowers
Decorating materials
Sticky tape

Bible link

Joshua 6

How to make it

1. Remove the paper tongue from the party blower and discard, leaving just the blower.

2. Decorate the coloured paper.

3. Roll the paper into a cone shape tightly around the blower. Cut to shape if necessary and fix in place using the sticky tape.

18 Jesus controls the weather: Weather chart

What you need

Large paper plate
Pictures symbolizing weather (cut out
 of magazines)
Glue
White card
Paper fastener

Bible link

'He replied, "You of little faith, why
are you so afraid?" Then he got up and
rebuked the winds and the waves, and
it was completely calm.'

Matthew 8:26

How to make it

1. Cut out pictures from magazines to represent different types of weather, such as someone holding an umbrella.

2. Stick them all round the edge of the paper plate.

3. Cut out an arrow from the card. It needs to be the size of the radius of the plate (from the centre to the edge).

4. Fasten the arrow using the paper fastener to the centre of the plate.

5. Children can now use the arrow to point to what the weather is at specific times.

19 Jesus turns water into wine: Stone water jar from clay

What you need

Air drying clay
Paint

Bible link

'Nearby stood six stone water jars, the kind used by the Jews for ceremonial washing, each holding from twenty to thirty gallons.'

John 2:6

How to make it

1. Roll the air dry clay into a long thin sausage.

2. Coil it round and round to make the shape of a pot. Squeeze the top into a spout shape.

3. Use a fatter roll of clay to make the handle. Leave to dry.

4. Paint the jar.

Note:
This is for decorative purposes only.

20 Jesus walks on the water: Paper boat

What you need

Paper
Decorating materials

Bible link

Jesus walks on water

Matthew 14

How to make it

1. Fold the paper in half from top to bottom.

2. Fold the paper in half from left to right.

3. Unfold the paper once.

4. Fold the top left tip over so that it touches the middle crease.

5. Turn the paper over.

6. Fold the other tip so it touches the middle crease.

7. Fold one bottom flap upwards and make a crease.

8. Turn the paper over.

9. Fold the other flap upwards and crease.

10. Insert both thumbs into the middle of the folded paper and pull outward. You should have a folded diamond shape.

11. Holding the diamond with the open side down, lift one bottom flap and make it touch the tip.

12. Turn the paper over and repeat step You should now have a triangle.

13. Insert both thumbs into the middle of the folded triangle and pull outward all the way.

14. Hold the two outer tips and pull all the way, flatten the paper.

15. Turn the boat upside down. Holding your fingers inside the boat, pull the sides out a little bit to make a wider base.

21 Jesus heals the sick: Get well cards

What you need

A5 card
Pens
Decorating materials

Bible link

'And wherever he went—into villages, towns or countryside—they placed the sick in the marketplaces. They begged him to let them touch even the edge of his cloak, and all who touched him were healed.'

Mark 6:56

How to make it

1. Fold the A5 card in half.

2. Write 'Get well soon' on the front of the card.

3. Decorate as wanted.

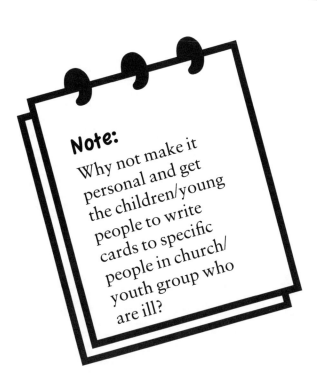

Note:
Why not make it personal and get the children/young people to write cards to specific people in church/ youth group who are ill?

22 Jesus washes disciples' feet: Fun soap

What you need

1 cup soap flakes
2 tablespoons hot water
Jelly moulds
Food colouring

Bible link

'After that, he poured water into a basin and began to wash his disciples' feet, drying them with the towel that was wrapped around him.'

John 13:5

How to make it

1. Mix the soap flakes and hot water in a pan till melted. (Warm over low heat if necessary.)

2. Add the food colouring till it is a strong colour.

3. Pour the liquid soap into the moulds and leave in a warm place to dry.

4. When the soap has dried remove it from the mould and place on a plate to harden. It may take several days to harden completely.

23 Palm Sunday: Palm tree

What you need

Cardboard tube from wrapping paper
Green paper
Sticky tape
Scissors

Bible link

'They took palm branches and went out to meet him, shouting, "Hosanna! Blessed is he who comes in the name of the Lord! Blessed is the King of Israel!"'

John 12:13

How to make it

1. Cut out lots of palm leaf shapes from the green paper.

2. Snip along the sides of all leaves.

3. Stick the leaves around the top of the tube.

24 Do not worry: Handprint lily

What you need

White paper
Pencil
3 yellow pipe cleaners
3 green pipe cleaners
Sticky tape
Ribbon

Bible link

Jesus tells people not to worry.
Matthew 6:25–34

How to make it

1. Draw round a child's hand three times.

2. Cut each one out.

3. Make a small loop at the top of one green pipe cleaner.

4. Thread yellow pipe cleaner through the loop and double over to make the flower centre.

5. Roll the paper hand around the green pipe cleaner to make the petals. Fix in place with sticky tape. Fold back the fingers.

6. Repeat steps 3 to 5 for the two remaining paper hands.

7. Group the flowers together and tie with a ribbon.

25 Running the race: Olympic torch

What you need

Cardboard tube from wrapping paper
Yellow card
Sticky tape
Glue
Silver foil

Bible link

'Therefore, since we are surrounded by such a great cloud of witnesses, let us throw off everything that hinders and the sin that so easily entangles, and let us run with perseverance the race marked out for us.'

Hebrews 12:1

How to make it

1. Cut out several flame shapes from the yellow card.

2. Tape the flames to the top of the cardboard tube.

3. Glue the silver foil over the whole of the cardboard tube.

26 Shield of faith: Paper mâché shield

What you need

1 large cardboard box
Paper mâché (see instructions in craft 97)
Silver acrylic paint
Newspaper
Masking tape

Bible link

'In addition to all this, take up the shield of faith, with which you can extinguish all the flaming arrows of the evil one.'

Ephesians 6:16

How to make it

1. Cut a large shield shape from the cardboard.

2. Roll the newspaper tightly and attach using masking tape in a cross shape on the back as a handle.

3. Cover the front in paper mâché.

4. Paint both sides of the shield in silver.

5. Decorate the front of the shield as required.

27 Shoes of readiness: Paper sandals

What you need

Card
Wool
Decorating materials

Bible link

'...with your feet fitted with the readiness that comes from the gospel of peace.'

Ephesians 6:15

How to make it

1. Place a pair of shoes on the card and draw round them.

2. Cut out the shoe outlines from the card.

3. Attach a length of wool from the bottom left of the shoeprint to just below the top right.

4. Attach a length of wool from the bottom right of the shoeprint to just below the top left.

5. Attach a length of wool from the top right to the top left.

6. The wool is the sandal straps.

7. Decorate the sandals as wanted.

28 Belt of truth: Circle belt

What you need

Card
Wool
Hole punch
Decorating materials

Bible link

'Stand firm then, with the belt of truth buckled around your waist.'

Ephesians 6:14

How to make it

1. Cut out lots of circles.

2. Punch two holes opposite each other in each circle.

3. Decorate all the circles.

4. Thread the circles onto a length of wool, using both holes so the circles lie flat.

5. Put the belt around the child's waist and tie it together at the front.

29 Sword of the Spirit: Foil sword

What you need

Card
Silver foil
Gold paint
Glue

Bible link

'Take the helmet of salvation and the sword of the Spirit, which is the word of God.'

Ephesians 6:17

How to make it

1. Cut out a sword shape from thick card.

2. Glue the silver foil over the blade of the sword.

3. Paint the handle gold and leave to dry.

30 Paul and Silas: Paul and Silas in prison

What you need

Picture of Paul and Silas in prison on A4 card
A4 card
Craft knife
Colouring pens
Glue

Bible link

Paul and Silas in prison
Acts 16:16–40

How to make it

1. Colour in the picture of Paul and Silas. (Older children could draw their own picture.)

2. Carefully using a craft knife cut out thin strips from the A4 card to make prison bars. (Adults may need to do this stage for younger children.)

3. Colour in the prison bars.

4. Stick the prison bars over the top of the picture of Paul and Silas.

31 Pentecost: Pentecost wreath

What you need

A4 pictures of different flags of the world
Card
Glue

Bible link

'Now there were staying in Jerusalem God-fearing Jews from every nation under heaven. When they heard this sound, a crowd came together in bewilderment, because each one heard them speaking in his own language.'

Acts 2:5–6

How to make it

1. Draw round a hand on lots of different flags and cut them out.

2. Stick them all together with the fingers facing out so that they make a complete circle.

3. Cut out a circle of card the same size as the gap in the middle of the hands.

4. Write a memory verse on the card and stick it in the centre of the wreath.

32 Paul 1: Paul's missionary passport

What you need

Photo of each child
A5 card
A5 paper
Glue

Bible link

Paul's missionary journeys
Acts 13–21

How to make it

1. If you are short on time it is a good idea to prepare the basic book in advance.

2. Make a small book with several pages in the middle (depending how many weeks you wish to use it).

3. On the front put your club name and logo, and the word 'passport'.

4. On the inside of the cover stick the child's photo. Write their name, address and date of birth etc.

5. As you look at the different places Paul visited, the children can get stamps to say they were present on those weeks.

33 Paul 2: Traveller's notebook

What you need

Spiral bound notebook with a plain
   matte cover
Lots of stamps (preferably foreign)
PVA glue
White sticker (optional)

Bible link

Paul's missionary journeys
Acts 13–21

How to make it

1. Cover the notebook front cover in a
thin layer of PVA glue.

2. Stick the stamps all over the cover.
They do not have to be in neat lines
and can overlap.

3. When you have completed the front
cover, turn over and repeat on the
back cover.

4. Trim the edges of the covers if
needed.

If you want you can put a sticker
on the front to identify the
notebook's owner.

34 Tithing: Money box

What you need

Small butter tub with lid
Decorating materials
Craft knife

Bible link

'God loves a cheerful giver.'
2 Corinthians 9:7b

How to make it

1. Cut a small slit in the top of the lid just bigger than the size of a coin.

2. Decorate the tub as wanted.

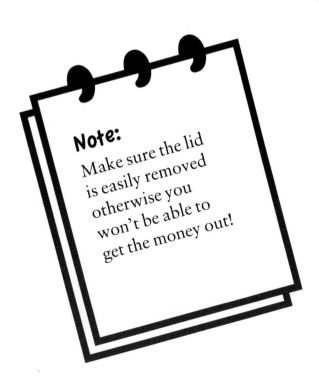

Note:
Make sure the lid is easily removed otherwise you won't be able to get the money out!

35 All nations: Chinese fan

What you need

A4 white paper
Decorating materials
2 wooden lollipop sticks
Glue

Bible link

'And they sang a new song: "You are worthy to take the scroll and to open its seals, because you were slain, and with you blood you purchased men for God from every tribe and language and people and nation."'

Revelation 5:9

How to make it

1. Decorate the paper on both sides.

2. Hold the piece of paper in front of you and fold the top forward about 2cm.

3. Turn the paper over and repeat. Fold all the way to the end of the paper. (It should look like a concertina when you have finished.)

4. Glue a lollipop stick onto each end of the fan, so a small bit is sticking out at the bottom of the paper.

5. Fold the paper open and you have a fan.

36 Fruit of the Spirit: Fruit of the Spirit picture

What you need

1 large piece of paper
Magazines
Glue

Bible link

'But the fruit of the Spirit is love, joy, peace, patience, kindness, goodness, faithfulness, gentleness and self-control.'

Galatians 5:22

How to make it

1. At the top of the piece of paper write 'The fruit of the Spirit is…'.

2. Get the children to search through the magazines looking for a picture that they think shows love.

3. Stick this on the paper and write love underneath.

4. Repeat until all the fruits have been represented.

37 The Lord's Supper: Remembrance poppy

What you need

A4 white paper
Pen
Glue
Red tissue paper
Black tissue paper

Bible link

'In the same way, after supper he took
the cup saying, "This cup is the new
covenant in my blood; do this, whenever
you drink it, in remembrance of me."'

1 Corinthians 11:25

How to make it

1. Draw the outline of a large poppy on
   the paper.

2. Screw up little balls of black tissue
   paper and make the centre of the
   flower.

3. Repeat the exercise with the red
   tissue paper for the petals.

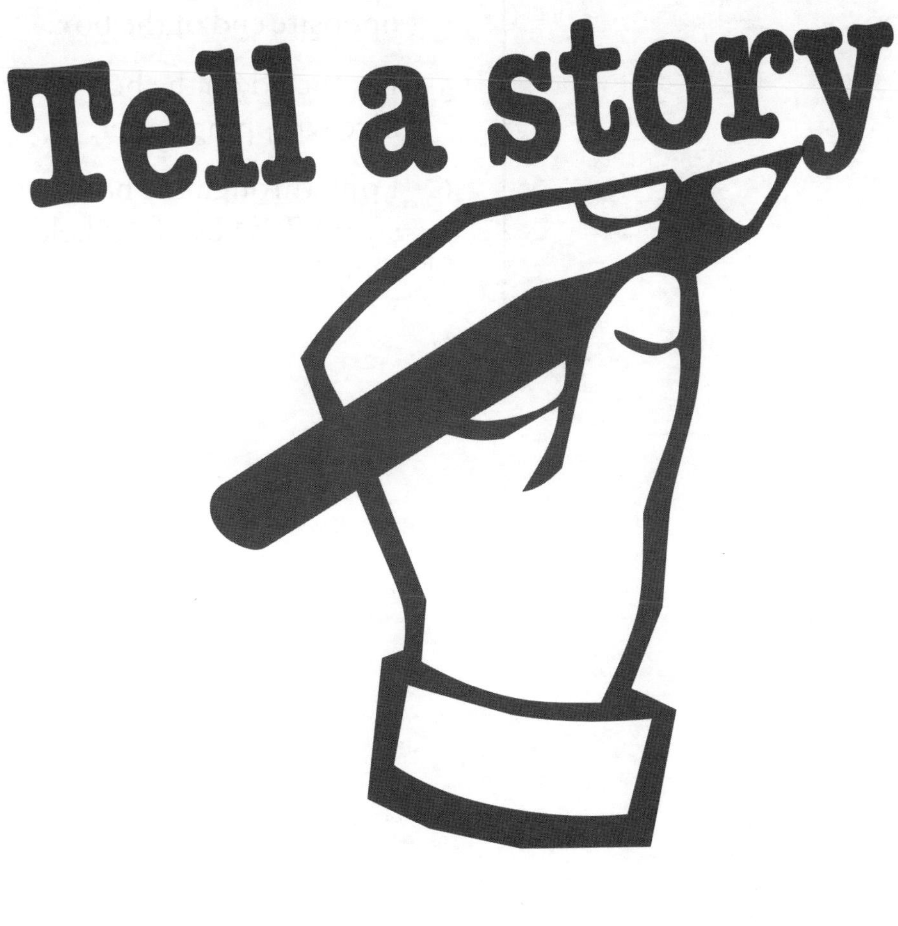
Tell a story

38 Shoebox show

What you need

Shoe box with lid
Paper
Glue
Scissors
Colouring pens
Wrapping paper

How to make it

1. Cut a piece of paper to the same size as the end of your shoe box. (The box should be held lengthways.)

2. Draw the story onto the paper.

3. Cut a square out of the end of the box then glue the picture in its place

4. Cut a small hole in the middle of the opposite end of the box.

5. Put the lid on the box and cover it in nice wrapping paper.

6. Look through the hole to see the story. (It's best if it's held up to the light.)

39 Light catcher picture

What you need

Photocopy of a Bible colouring picture (these can be found in books or on the Internet)
Acetates (suitable for use on a photocopier or printer)
PVA glue
Paint

How to make it

1. Print the picture onto acetate.

2. Mix a small amount of PVA glue with the paint.

3. Paint the picture and leave it to dry.

4. Stick on your window as a light catcher.

40 My story Bible

What you need

2 sheets of A4 Card
A4 paper
Paper fasteners
Colouring pens

How to make it

1. Decide how many stories will be in your Bible. (You could make this a term's project.)

2. Place the correct number of sheets of paper between the two sheets of card and fasten with two paper fasteners.

3. On the front write the title and heading, and the child's name.

4. On each subsequent page draw a picture of the story with the memory verse underneath.

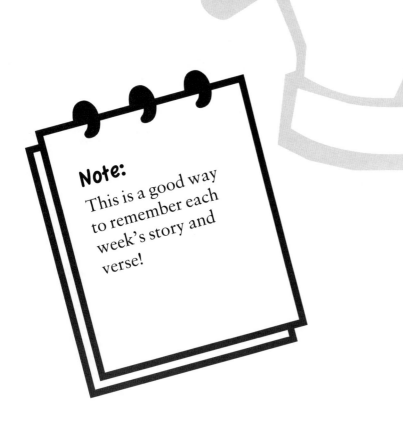

Note:
This is a good way to remember each week's story and verse!

41 Pasta picture

What you need

A4 card
Pasta (variety of types and shapes)
Paint

How to make it

1. Use the pasta shapes to create a picture.

2. Glue the pasta into place on the card.

3. Paint the picture and leave to dry.

42 Jigsaw

What you need

Card
Scissors
Pens

How to make it

1. Draw your favourite Bible story onto the card and colour in.

2. Once your picture is finished make a photocopy of it to be a guide.

3. Cut the original picture into jigsaw shapes.

4. If you have time then you can make a small box to store the jigsaw.

43 Shell picture

What you need

Paper
Shells
Glue

How to make it

1. In advance you will need to collect lots of shells and gently break them into small pieces.

2. Get each child to draw a picture of the story on the card.

3. Instead of colouring the picture, cover it in glue and use the shell pieces to fill in the colour.

44 Mobiles

What you need

Wire coat hanger
String
Sticky tape
Card
Colouring pens

How to make it

1. Decide how many scenes are in your story.

2. Cut out that number of circles from card.

3. Draw a scene on each circle. Draw the same picture on the reverse of the circle.

4. Attach string to the circle and tie onto a wire coat hanger.

5. Repeat the same for each scene.

Memory verses

45 Memory verse placemat

What you need

A4 paper
Colouring pens
Glue
Decorating materials, such as
 glitter, etc.
Access to a laminator

How to make it

1. Write out the memory verse in large letters. (For younger children this can be printed out in advance.)

2. Colour in and decorate.

3. When the glue has dried laminate each sheet of paper.

Note:
For a smaller craft and short memory verse you can use the same principle to make coasters.

46 Heart box

What you need

Thick card
Choice of memory verse
Glue
Decorating materials
Paper ribbon
Sweets or chocolates (optional)

Bible link

'Man looks at the outward appearance, but the LORD looks at the heart.'

1 Samuel 16:7b

How to make it

1. Using the example below, draw your basic heart box onto thick card.

2. Write the memory verse onto the front of the card.

3. Decorate it.

4. Cut out along the solid lines and fold along the dotted lines.

5. Glue tabs 1 and 2 together.

6. Make small holes at the top of the heart and loop through some paper ribbon to make handle.

7. Put some sweets inside.

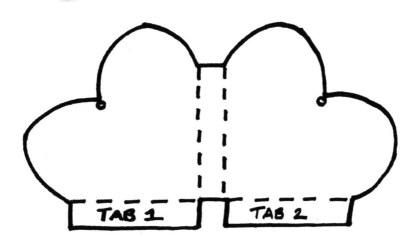

TAB 1   TAB 2

47 Foam door hanger

What you need

Foam sheets
Self adhesive foam letters
Craft knife

How to make it

1. Cut a long piece of foam (about ½ A4 sheet folded lengthways).

2. Using a craft knife cut out a hole big enough to fit a handle through. (You may wish to do this yourself.)

3. Using foam letters write out memory verse.

48 Bookmarks

What you need

Thick card
Decorating materials
Colouring pens

How to make it

1. Cut out an oblong shape about the size of a standard bookmark.

2. Write out memory verse.

3. Decorate as wanted.

49 Glittery framed verse

What you need

Paper
Untreated wooden frame
Colouring pens
Glitter glue

How to make it

1. On a piece of paper (same size as the frame) write out the memory verse.

2. Place inside frame.

3. Decorate the wooden frame using glitter glue.

50 Globe verse

What you need

Card

Lots of pictures of people of all
nationalities and ages cut out of
magazines

Glue

Pen

Sticky tape

String

Bible link

'For God so loved the world that he
gave his one and only Son, that
whoever believes in him shall not
perish but have eternal life.'

John 3:16

How to make it

1. Cut out a large circle of card.

2. Cover the card in pictures (collage
   style) of people and glue in place.

3. On a piece of white paper write out
   the memory verse and stick over the
   top of the collage.

4. Make a loop of string and tape to the
   top of the card at the back.

Note:
For a slightly
longer craft repeat
the same on the
back.

51 New Year calendar

What you need

A4 coloured card
Small calendars
Decorating materials
Sticky tape
String

How to make it

1. Write out the memory verse on the card.

2. Glue a small calendar to the bottom of the card.

3. Decorate as wanted.

4. Make loop of string and tape to back.

Note:
Why not use your church's verse for the year?

52 Paper chain verse

What you need

Strips of paper
Colouring pens
Glue

How to make it

1. Count how many words, including the Bible reference, are in your memory verse.

2. Cut out the same number of paper strips.

3. Write one word on each strip and decorate.

4. Make the first strip into a loop using glue to secure. Link each strip together gluing into place.

Note: You could make this a Christmas activity.

53 Craft T-shirt

What you need

White T-shirt
Fabric pens

How to make it

1. Write out the memory verse onto the T-shirt.

2. Decorate the back with appropriate pictures.

Note: Different fabric pens require different processes so read the instructions carefully before you start.

54 Pencil pot

What you need

Tubs (Instant gravy tubs work well)
Self adhesive foam sheets
Self adhesive foam shapes, letters and
   numbers

How to make it

1. Cut a foam rectangle the same width and length as the tub you are using.

2. Stick the rectangle around the tub so it is completely covered.

3. Using the foam shapes, letters and numbers decorate with the memory verse.

55 Group collage

What you need

Large sheet of white card
Paint
Pen

Bible link

'"Come, follow me," Jesus said, "and I will make you fishers of men."'

Mark 1:17

How to make it

1. Cover a child's foot with coloured paint.

2. Make a clear footprint mark on the card.

3. Repeat for each child.

4. Wait for the collage to dry.

5. Over each foot write a word from the memory verse.

56 Bible verse mosaic

What you need

Paper (cut into lots of different shapes)
Pens
Large sheet of paper
Glue

How to make it

1. Give each child a piece of paper.

2. Each child should write out and illustrate a Bible verse they have learnt. Try and get everyone to do a different verse.

3. Stick them all up on a large sheet of paper so they can see how many Bible verses they have learnt.

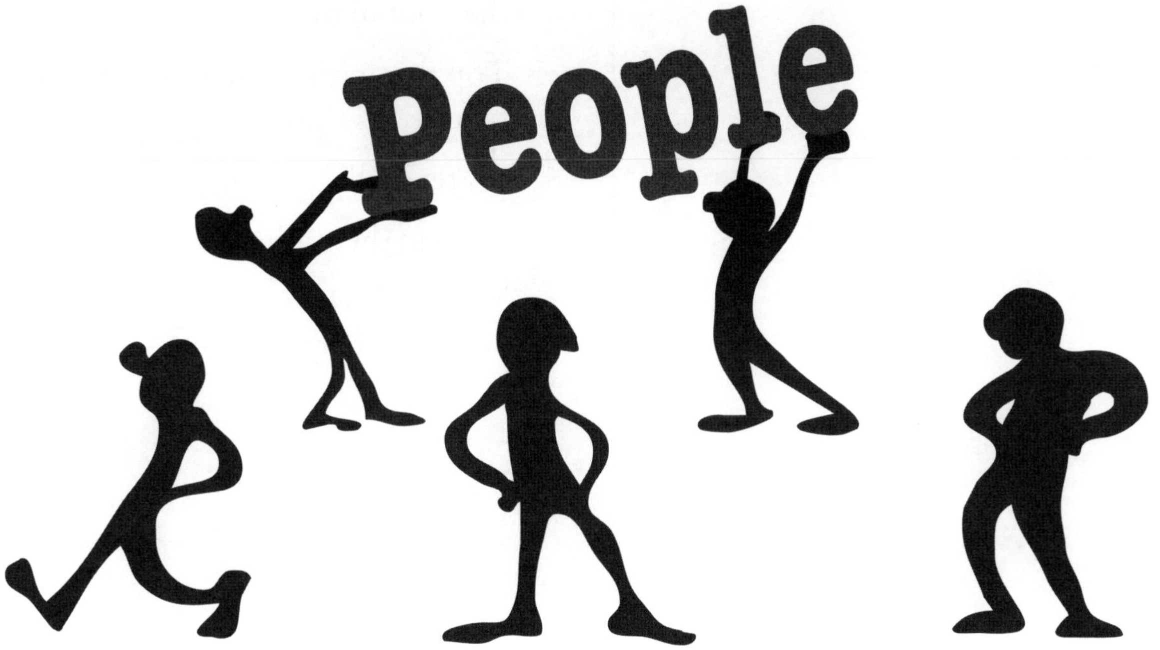
People

57 Grass heads

What you need

9oz plastic cup
1 cup potting soil
1 tablespoon grass seeds
Stickers for decoration

How to make it

1. Decorate the plastic cup so it looks like a face.

2. Fill the cup halfway with soil.

3. Divide the remaining soil in two.

4. Mix the grass seeds with half the soil then put in the cup.

5. Top this with the remaining soil (about ¼" thick).

6. Water well.

7. Keep in the sunlight and water as necessary.

8. Give him/her a haircut!

58 Peg doll

What you need

Wooden clothespin
Wool
Black colouring pen
Material
Pipe cleaner

How to make it

1. Draw a face on the head of the clothespin.

2. Glue the wool onto the head of the clothespin to make hair.

3. Wrap the pipe cleaner around clothespin to make the arms and fold the ends slightly to make hands.

4. Cut a rectangle out of the material, fold in half and cut a small hole in the fold.

5. Place the material over the head of the clothespin to make a tunic, tie a piece of wool around the middle of the tunic to keep the tunic closed.

59 Wooden spoon people

What you need

Wooden spoon
Glue
Wool
Buttons
Marker pen
Material (optional)
Pipe cleaners (optional)

How to make it

1. Glue the wool to the top of the spoon to make hair.

2. Glue the buttons on to make eyes.

3. Using the marker pen draw a nose and mouth.

4. For a slightly more adventurous spoon person, use the pipe cleaners to make arms and legs, and use the material to make clothes.

60 Lollipop stick people

What you need

Wooden lollipop sticks
Colouring pens
Wool
Felt
Glue

How to make it

1. Draw a face on one side of the lollipop stick at the top.

2. Glue on some wool as hair.

3. Cut a simple dress, trousers or top outline and glue onto centre of lollipop stick.

61 Kitchen roll people

What you need

Kitchen roll tube (cut to the same
  length as a toilet roll)
Cereal box
Coloured crepe paper
Glue
Colouring pens
Wool

How to make it

1. Cut out two arms and hands, two
   feet and a face from the cereal box

2. Cover the toilet roll in crepe paper
   and glue it into place. This makes the
   body.

3. Cover the arms and legs in crepe
   paper and glue into place.

4. Attach the arms and legs to the body
   with glue.

5. Draw eyes, nose and mouth onto the
   face and glue on hair using the wool.
   Colour in as necessary.

6. Stick the face on the front of the
   toilet roll.

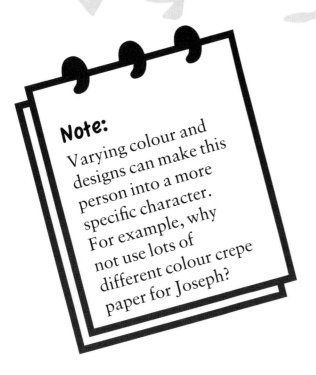

Note:
Varying colour and
designs can make this
person into a more
specific character.
For example, why
not use lots of
different colour crepe
paper for Joseph?

62 Paper chain dolls

What you need

Thick paper
Scissors
Colouring pens
Glue
Decorating materials (examples below):
    Scraps of paper and fabric
    Buttons
    Glitter
    Silver foil
    Stickers

How to make it

1. Cut a strip of paper about 10cm high. It can be as long as you like, depending on how many dolls you are making.

2. Fold the paper in an accordion style, with each section being about 6cm wide.

3. Draw a person onto the top section using the template. Make sure that the head, arms and feet touch the sides at some point.

4. Cut out the shape, but do not cut along the folds.

5. Unfold the dolls. You should have a strip of dolls holding hands.

6. Decorate each individual doll.

Note:
Why not make twelve disciples?

Example

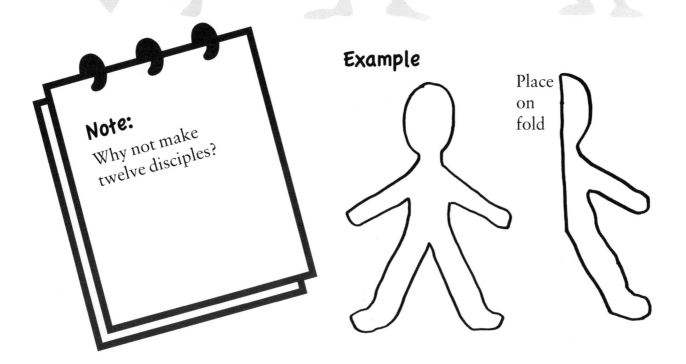

Place on fold

63 Pipe cleaner people

What you need

4 pipe cleaners per child
Googly eyes
Pencil
Craft glue
Scissors

How to make it

1. Make an upside-down V shape with the pipe cleaner and twist a small loop at the top.

2. Twist the two ends together a few times to make the body.

3. Coil a second pipe cleaner around a standard pencil.

4. Slide this over the body. (If it is too long you can cut down the coiled section.)

5. Slide a third pipe cleaner through the loop for the arms. (Cut down if necessary.)

6. Tightly wrap a fourth pipe cleaner over a pencil, going over the top of its self to make a round head.

7. Glue the head onto the top of the loop.

8. Slightly bend the end of the arms and legs to make hands and feet.

9. Glue googly eyes to the head to make a face.

Animals

64 Flannel soap fish

What you need

Flannel
Small bar of soap
Rubber band
Ribbon
Self adhesive foam sheets

Bible link

'And God said, "Let the water teem with living creatures."'

Genesis 1:20a

How to make it

1. Place the flannel on the table with one corner pointing towards you.

2. Place the soap in the centre of the flannel.

3. Gather all of the corners together at the end of the bar of soap and secure with the rubber band. (The corners should now form the fish tail.)

4. Cut out eyes, fins and a mouth from the self adhesive foam and stick them onto the flannel.

5. Tie the ribbon around the rubber band.

6. You now have a fish!

65 Jonah in the big fish

What you need

Small clear plastic bottle
Foam sheets
Pipe cleaners
Googly eyes
Glue

Bible link

'But the LORD provided a great fish to swallow Jonah, and Jonah was inside the fish three days and three nights.'
Jonah 1:17

How to make it

1. Cut out tail, fins and mouth from the foam.

2. Make a small pipe cleaner man and place inside bottle, then screw the lid on tightly.

3. Attach googly eyes on either side of bottle neck. The bottle lid becomes the nose.

4. Glue the mouth, tail and fins onto the bottle.

66 Fishing nets

What you need

Net (the type you get your fruit in at the supermarket)
Paper
Pens
Straw

Bible link

'[Jesus] said, "Throw your net on the right side of the boat and you will find some." When they did, they were unable to haul the net in because of the large number of fish.'

John 21:6

How to make it

1. Cut out lots of fish shapes from paper and decorate them. (Each child should make as many fish as possible.)

2. Place the fish into the net through the hole.

3. Gather the net together and tape up the hole attaching a straw as a pole to hold the net. (You could always use string instead of a straw.)

67 Sheep 1: Lamb note holders

What you need

White card
Black card
2 Clothes pegs (the spring-operated kind)
Glue
Googly eyes
Cotton wool

Bible link

'Tell the whole community of Israel that on the tenth day of this month each man is to take a lamb for his family, one for each household.'

Exodus 12:3

How to make it

1. Cut a circle out of the white card about 3" in diameter

2. Cover the circle of card in cotton wool.

3. Draw a picture of a sheep face on the black card, cut out and stick to the circle.

4. Stick the googly eyes onto the black card.

5. Glue the two pegs upside down to the back of the card.

6. The pegs can now be used to hold notes.

7. These are now freestanding.

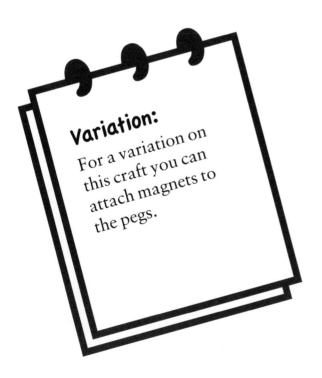

Variation:
For a variation on this craft you can attach magnets to the pegs.

68 Sheep 2: Cotton wool sheep picture

What you need

A4 white card
Cotton wool
Marker pen
Googly eyes

Bible link

'And there were shepherds living out in the fields nearby, keeping watch over their flocks at night.'

Luke 2:8

How to make it

1. Draw a sheep outline on the white card.

2. Cover the body of the sheep in cotton wool.

3. Draw on a mouth and colour in the legs.

4. Attach googly eyes.

69 Sheep 3: Pom-pom sheep

What you need

Large white pom-pom
Black card
Googly eyes
Glue

Bible link

The parable of the lost sheep
Matthew 18:12–14

How to make it

1. Cut a square of card slightly larger than the pom-pom.

2. Glue the pom-pom onto the card.

3. Cut the outline of a sheep's face out of black card.

4. Stick on two googly eyes.

5. Attach the face to the front of the pom-pom.

70 Bird feeders

What you need

Plastic 1 litre bottle
Craft knife
2 wooden spoons
Birdseed
Strong string
Mug hook

Bible link

'Look at the birds of the air; they do not sow or reap or store away in barns, and yet your heavenly Father feeds them. Are you not much more valuable than they?'

Matthew 6:26

How to make it

1. About 4 inches from the bottom of the bottle draw a small circle the same size as the wooden spoon handle, rotate the bottle 180° and do the same on the other side. Make sure the holes line up.

2. Using a craft knife, cut out the small circles. (This step may need to be carried out by a responsible adult.)

3. Insert a wooden spoon through the two holes.

4. Repeat the process further up the bottle.

5. Screw the mug hook into the bottle lid.

6. Fill the bottle with birdseed.

7. Tie the string to the hook and replace the lid on the bottle.

8. Hang your birdfeeder somewhere in the garden.

71 Polystyrene egg bird

What you need

Polystyrene egg
Double-sided tape
Feathers
Googly eyes
Felt

Bible link

'How majestic is your name in all the earth.'

Psalm 8:1

How to make it

1. Put the egg on the table with the pointy end up.

2. Put two strips of double-sided tape around the egg.

3. Stick as many feathers on as you can.

4. Fix on googly eyes.

5. Cut a diamond shape out of the felt, fold in half and stick onto the egg to make a beak.

6. Cut out a heart shape from the felt and stick to the bottom of the egg to make feet.

72 Paper bag raven

What you need

Paper bag
Black paint
Colouring pens
Glue
Thick black paper
Yellow foam sheets
White paper

Bible link

'The ravens brought [Elijah] bread and meat in the morning and bread and meat in the evening, and he drank from the brook.'

1 Kings 17:6

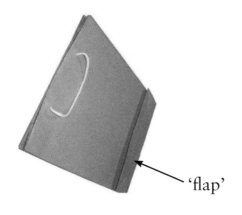

'flap'

How to make it

1. Place the paper bag on the table. The flap should be at the top and facing up. Cut off the handles.

2. Paint the bag black and leave to dry.

3. While the bag is drying, cut out wings and a tail from the black paper.

4. Cut out a beak and feet from the yellow foam sheets.

5. Cut out two circles from the white paper and two slightly smaller from the black paper for the eyes.

6. When the bag is dry you can begin to assemble.

7. Slip the wings into the side flaps and glue into place.

8. Glue the tail onto the back of the bag.

9. Attach feet to the bottom of the bag. (It's neater if they are glued to the inside, but do not glue the bag shut!)

10. Glue the eyes and the beak to the top of the top flap.

11. The child can now place their hand into the bag and use it as a puppet.

73 Egg box camel

What you need

1 egg carton
Brown paint
Masking tape or glue
Googly eyes
4 wooden pegs

Bible link

Rebekah at the well

Genesis 24:1–24

How to make it

1. Cut out two of the base sections (leaving them joined together).

2. Attach the pegs to the base sections as legs using masking tape or glue.

3. Cut out a strip from the discarded egg box to make the neck.

4. Attach one of the base sections to the neck and join it to the body using masking tape or glue.

5. Cut another short strip for the tail and attach it to the body.

6. Paint the camel brown and leave to dry.

7. When the paint has dried fix two googly eyes to the head.

74 Paper dove

What you need

Templates (pages 91–93)
4 sheets of A4 Paper
Colouring pens
Stapler
String

Bible link

'As soon as Jesus was baptized, he went up out of the water. At that moment heaven was opened, and he saw the Spirit of God descending like a dove and lighting on him. And a voice from heaven said, "This is my Son, whom I love; with him I am well pleased."'

Matthew 3:16–17

How to make it

1. Using the templates included, copy onto A4 Paper.

2. Decorate.

3. Cut out the four templates along the solid lines.

4. Fold the tail into a concertina like a fan.

5. Insert the tail into the slit on the dove's body and staple to secure.

6. Staple the wings onto the body.

7. Attach the string to the head and hang as a mobile.

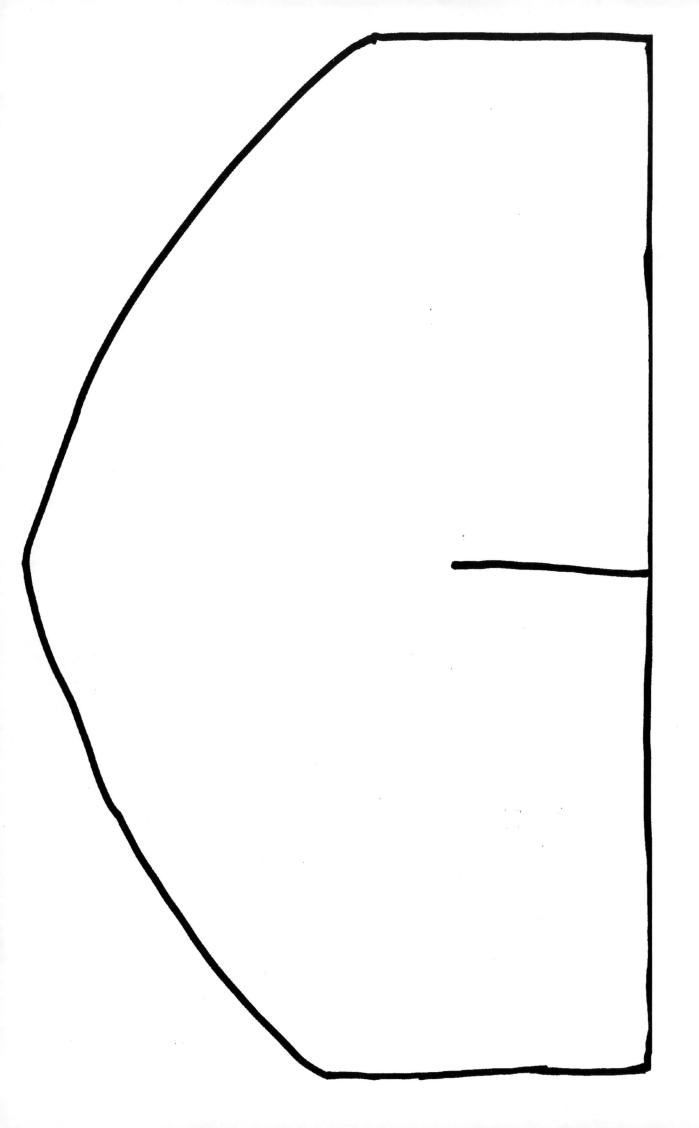

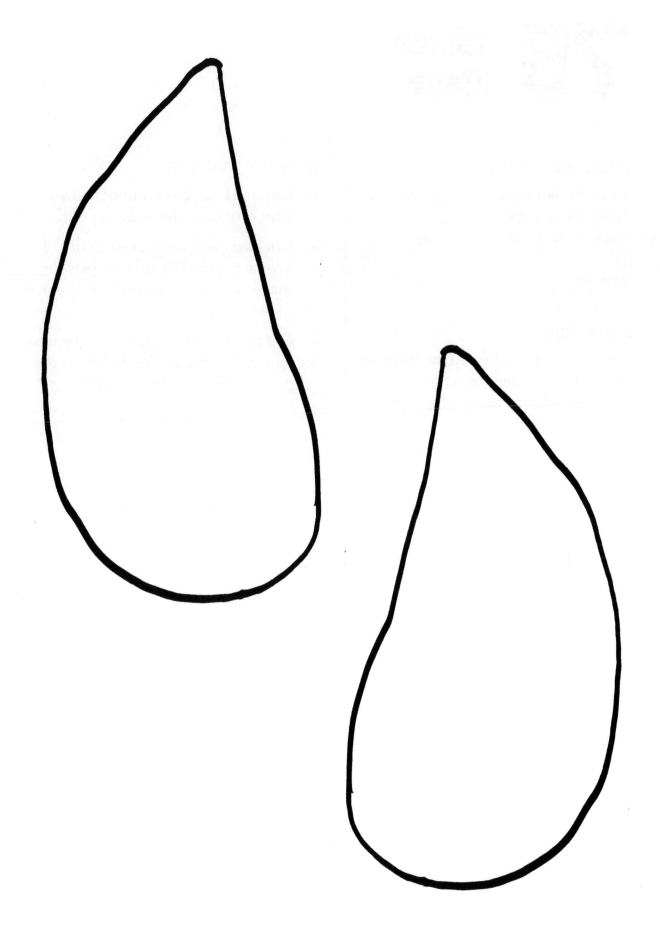

75 Circle Bear

What you need

Thick brown paper
Thick white paper
Black marker pen
Glue
Scissors

Bible link

'The LORD who delivered me from the paw of the lion and the paw of the bear will deliver me from the hand of this Philistine.'

1 Samuel 17:37

How to make it

1. Cut one large circle out of brown paper to make the body.

2. Cut two medium circles out of brown paper. The first circle is for the head. Cut the second circle in half to make the feet.

3. Cut three small circles out of brown paper. Use two of the circles for the paws and cut the third in half to make ears.

4. Glue the circles together onto the white paper to make the bear.

5. Cut several small white circles to decorate the paws, ears and tummy.

6. Use the pen to draw on a face.

76 Lion mask

What you need

Paper dinner plate
Sharp scissors
Craft glue
Golden-brown wool
Marker pen
Elastic cord

Bible link

'Samson went down to Timnah together with his father and mother. As they approached the vineyards of Timnah, suddenly a young lion came roaring towards him. The Spirit of the LORD came upon him in power so that he tore the lion apart with his bare hands as he might have torn a young goat. But he told neither his father nor his mother what he had done.'

Judges 14:5–6

How to make it

1. Use sharp scissors to cut out eye holes in the paper plate.

2. Draw a lion's face on the plate and colour it in.

3. Glue wool around the edge of the plate to make a mane.

4. Make two small holes on either side of the mask and attach elastic cord to hold mask in place.

77 Balloon pig

What you need

Pink balloon
Bottom section of egg carton
Pink paper ribbon
Pink paint
Marker pen
Scissors
Googly eyes
Glue

Bible link

The parable of the prodigal son
Luke 15:11-32

How to make it

1. Cut the egg carton into sections of four egg cups and paint pink.

2. Blow up the balloon.

3. Make the tie-off point the nose and attach googly eyes just above the nose.

4. Draw on a mouth just below the nose.

5. Curl some pink paper ribbon and glue on as a tail.

6. When the egg carton segments are dry, glue on as feet.

78 Fingerprint butterfly

What you need

A4 white paper
Pencil
Paint (variety of colours)
Coloured card
Scissors
Glue
Marker pen

Bible link

'For you have been born again, not of perishable seed, but of imperishable, through the living and enduring word of God.'

1 Peter 1:23

How to make it

1. Fold the A4 paper in half.

2. Draw half a butterfly using the fold as the centre.

3. Paint half the butterfly using your fingers.

4. While the paint is still wet, fold the paper over and press down firmly.

5. Cut out the butterfly using the outline of the original half. Open the paper up and then leave to dry.

6. Glue onto a coloured piece of card.

7. Write a memory verse underneath (optional).

79 Pencil chicken

What you need

Yellow colouring pencil
Yellow feather
Yellow foam sheets
Yellow pipe cleaner
Googly eyes
Glue

How to make it

1. Place the feather at the top and back of the pencil with lots of the feather showing.

2. Hold firmly in place and wrap the pipe cleaner around the pencil spiralling downwards.

3. At the top and front of the pencil stick on googly eyes.

4. Cut a beak from the yellow foam sheets and glue in place just below the eyes.

80 Paper plate frog

What you need

Green card
Egg carton
Paper plate
Green paint
Masking tape
Red ribbon
Black marker pen

Bible link

'I will plague your whole country with frogs.'

Exodus 8:2

How to make it

1. Fold the paper plate in half with the fold at the back.

2. Cut two individual sections from the egg carton.

3. Attach the two egg carton sections to the top using masking tape. These are the eyes.

4. Paint the outside of the plate and egg carton sections green. Leave to dry.

5. Cut out two arms and two legs from the green card.

6. Glue the arms and legs to the plate.

7. Open the mouth and attach the ribbon as a tongue.

8. Using black marker pen draw on the eyes.

81 Egg carton caterpillar

What you need

Bottom section of egg carton
Paper fasteners
1 pipe cleaner
Googly eyes
Paint

Bible link

Psalm 78

How to make it

1. Cut out as many individual egg cups as you like (the more you use the longer the caterpillar).

2. Attach them together in a line using the paper fasteners.

3. Put two small holes in the top of the first one.

4. Cut the pipe cleaner in half and poke through the holes. Curl them to make the antennas.

5. Stick the googly eyes onto the cup and draw on a mouth.

6. Decorate the caterpillar with the paint.

82 Simple origami dog

What you need

Square of paper
Colouring pens

Bible link

The rich man and Lazarus
Luke 16:19–31

How to make it

1. Fold the paper in half diagonally. Keep the point facing towards you.

2. Fold two narrow corner triangles down towards you. A gap should be left at the top so the triangles don't touch. The triangles are the ears.

3. Draw a dog's face on the large section and decorate.

83 Creative creatures

What you need

A selection of 'junk' —suggested ideas below:
- Egg cartons
- Kitchen roll tubes
- Plastic bottles
- Boxes
- Crafty bits
- Googly eyes
- Pipe cleaners
- Coloured paper and card
- Self adhesive foam sheets
- Crepe paper

Other
- Glue
- Scissors
- Colouring pens

Bible link

'You are to bring into the ark two of all living creatures, male and female, to keep them alive with you.'

Genesis 6:19

How to make it

1. Encourage the children to use their imaginations to make one of God's creatures; it could be a bird, animal or fish.

84 Sock puppets

What you need

1 sock
Fabric glue
Cereal box
Felt
Googly eyes
Any other decorative bits

Bible link

'And God said, "Let the land produce living creatures according to their kinds: livestock, creatures that move along the ground, and wild animals, each according to its kind." And it was so.'

Genesis 1:24

How to make it

1. These are instructions for making the basic puppet. This can then be decorated to make any animal of your choice.

2. Cut out the basic mouth pattern (size depends on sock size) from cereal box card.

3. Fold along the middle and insert into the sock. The fold should fit into your hand when your hand is in the sock.

4. Depending on the animal you're making and the sock shape, you may wish to cut away excess bits of material and glue the 'mouth' into place to make it neater.

5. Decorate the sock to make your animal.

85 Animal masks

What you need

Thick cereal boxes
Scissors
Animal print paper (optional)
Colouring pens
Elastic cord

Bible link

'God made the wild animals according to their kinds, the livestock according to their kinds, and all the creatures that move along the ground according to their kinds. And God saw that it was good.'

Genesis 1:25

How to make it

1. Draw the outline of an animal's head on the cereal box. (For younger children you may wish to do this in advance.)

2. Using sharp scissors cut out eye holes.

3. Decorate as wanted, using the animal print paper and colouring pens.

4. Make two small holes on either side of the mask.

5. Attach elastic cord to hold mask in place.

86 King or Queen crown

What you need

Card
Scissors
Decorating materials
Colouring pens
Sticky tape

How to make it

1. Before starting the craft measure a child's head and cut the card to the right length.

2. Cut the top of the card into crown points.

3. Decorate the crown with jewels.

4. Stick the two ends together using sticky tape.

87 Treasure chest

What you need

Shoe box with lid
Masking tape
Black and yellow paint
Red material
Yellow card or paper
Scissors
Glue
Jewels (optional)

How to make it

1. Along each edge of the box place masking tape.

2. Paint the rest of the box black and leave to dry.

3. Remove the masking tape and fill in the gaps with yellow paint and leave to dry.

4. Cover the inside of the box with red material and glue it in carefully.

5. Cut a lock shape out of yellow card and glue it to the front of the box.

6. Cover the box in jewels (optional).

88 Scroll

What you need

Paper
Colouring pens
Ribbon

How to make it

1. Write a Bible verse on the paper. Draw a picture which links to the Bible verse and decorate the paper.

2. Roll up the paper and tie with a ribbon.

89 Drum

What you need

Small yogurt pot with lid (or similar
   plastic container)
Paint
Dried beans or pulses
Glue
Decorating materials

How to make it

1. Paint the container and leave to dry.

2. Decorate the outside of the
   container.

3. Fill the container about a quarter full
   of dried beans or pulses.

4. Put a bit of glue around the edge of
   the lid and put it on tightly. Leave the
   glue to dry.

90 Bath salts

What you need

Epsom salts
Coarse salt
Large jar with lid
Food colouring
Scented oil
Small piece of fabric (2–3cm bigger
    than the lid of the jar)
Elastic band

How to make it

1. In a large bowl, mix 2 cups of Epsom salts with 1 cup of coarse salt.

2. Stir in 2–3 drops of food colouring.

3. Stir in 5–6 drops of scented oil.

4. Pour the finished bath salts into the jar and put on a lid.

5. Put a square of fabric over the lid and secure with an elastic band.

91 Peppermint creams

What you need

9oz icing sugar
½ egg white
1 teaspoon peppermint flavouring
2 teaspoons lemon juice
Food colouring

How to make it

1. Sift 9oz of icing sugar into a bowl and make a small dip in the middle.

2. Add the egg white, lemon juice and peppermint flavouring.

3. Mix well using a knife to begin with. (As it gets stiffer you may need to use your hands.)

4. Separate the mixture into several sections depending on how many colours you have.

5. Add a drop of food colouring to each section.

6. Mix well and make into whatever shape you want.

Note:
Why not make loaves and fishes?

Dried egg white can be bought if you do not wish to use fresh.

92 Paper lanterns

What you need

Bright coloured A4 paper
Pencil
Sticky tape
Felts
Ruler
Scissors

How to make it

1. Using the ruler, measure about 1 ruler's width along the short edge of the paper and cut off to make the handle.

2. Fold the piece of paper in half lengthwise, making sure you line up the edges. At this stage the best side should be inside.

3. Draw a line ¾" in along the open edge.

4. At the folded edge cut up short wise to meet the line you drew on the open edge.

5. All along the folded edge make cuts 1inch apart

6. Unfold and refold the paper so that the best side is outwards.

7. Decorate the outside of the lamp.

8. To assemble, roll the lantern short wise to make a cylindrical shape and tape the edges together.

9. Push the two ends to the centre to make the folds bulge out and give it some shape.

10. Tape the handle to the top.

93 Tea light holders

What you need

Tea lights
Small glasses (make sure they are
   suitable to put tea lights in)
Pens or paints for decorating glass

How to make it

1. This simple craft gives children plenty of creative opportunities.

2. Decorate the glasses however you wish.

3. Place a tea light inside.

94 Badges

What you need

Card
Sticky tape
Decorating materials
Safety pins

How to make it

1. Cut out a small shape from the card. Traditionally badges are a circle but this is not essential!

2. Decorate as wanted.

3. For extra durability you could laminate the badges.

4. Fix a safety pin to the back of the card with sticky tape.

95 Cards

What you need

A5 card
Envelopes
Decorating materials
Colouring pens

How to make it

1. This is a simple craft but always popular.

2. Fold the A5 card in half.

3. Decorate as wanted.

4. Write a Bible verse inside.

5. Put the card in an envelope.

96 No cooking playdough

What you need

1 cup salt
1 cup flour
1 tablespoon cooking oil
Food colouring
Water

How to make it

1. Mix the salt and flour together thoroughly.

2. Add the oil and mix.

3. Mix in water as needed until you reach the right consistency.

4. Add a drop of food colouring and mix together until the colour is throughout the dough.

Note:
The playdough must be kept in an airtight container so that it does not dry out.

97 Paper mâché

What you need

Lots of newspaper
Toilet paper
PVA glue
Water

How to make it

1. Tear newspaper and toilet paper into strips.

2. Mix the glue with water (3 parts glue to 1 part water).

3. Cover whatever you are making in a layer of glue and then overlapping strips of newspaper and toilet paper. It does not have to be neat and tidy!

4. Keep repeating step 3 until it is the thickness you want. The more layers, the thicker and stronger it will be.

5. Leave to dry completely before painting or decorating.

98 Biscuit decorating

What you need

Plain biscuits, such as rich tea
Icing sugar
Water
Sweets

How to make it

1. Make up the icing as instructed on the icing sugar box. It needs to be a thick consistency.

2. Cover the biscuit in icing.

3. Decorate with sweets and leave to set.

99 Easy fridge magnets

What you need

Foam sheets
Magnetic self adhesive strips
Scissors
Decorating materials
Glue

How to make it

1. Cut a shape from the foam which relates to the theme of your craft.

2. Decorate the shape.

3. Attach the magnetic strip to the back of the foam.

4. The magnet can now be stuck to the fridge or other magnetic surface.

100 Star table decoration

What you need

Thick paper
Pencil
Scissors
Decorating materials

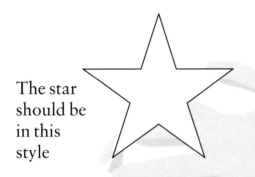

The star
should be
in this
style

How to make it

1. Draw a star shape on the thick paper and cut it out.

2. Take a second piece of paper and make a second star the same size (use the first as a template).

3. Decorate the stars on both sides.

4. Take the first star and cut a slit from point 1 to the centre.

5. Take the second star and cut a slit from point 2 to the centre.

6. Slip the two stars together using the slits.

7. You may wish to use tape for additional stability.

101 Microwave ornaments

What you need

4 cups flour
1 cup salt
1 to 1½ cups hot water
Christmas cookie cutters
Decorating materials, such as glitter,
    paint, beads etc.
Pin
Ribbon

How to make it

1. Mix the flour and salt together.

2. Add water gradually until you reach
    a stiff consistency.

3. Using a rolling pin, roll the dough
    out until it's about ½ cm thick.

4. Use the Christmas cutters to cut out
    shapes in the dough. Make a hole at
    the top of the shape with a pin; it
    needs to be big enough for the ribbon
    to be threaded through.

5. Put the shapes on a microwaveable
    plate and microwave on a low heat.
    It takes about 4 minutes, but increase
    slowly in 1 minute bursts so that you
    can keep a close eye on them.

6. Decorate the ornament.

7. Tie the ribbon through to make a
    hanging loop.

Index

Also available

Games, games, more games!

101 great ideas for youth clubs

TIRZAH L JONES

128PP, PAPERBACK

ISBN 978-1-84625-168-9

Do you ever find yourself planning your youth work and struggling to think of games? Or have you got tired of using the same old games, and do you long for some fresh ideas? It's easy to find resources with ideas for crafts, activities and talks, but what about those times when all you want are ideas for games?

Tirzah L Jones has been involved with youth work all her life and here she has collected together 101 games that are suitable for groups of all ages and situations. The organization of the games (into categories and according to age range) means that this resource is easy to use and you can find just the right game for your group. Useful tips are included to help you add variety to the games, as well as to help them fit in with a particular Bible theme you may be running.

'This little book is a resource that all who work with children and young people will find invaluable and great fun for the groups they work with.'

—Gareth James, minister in Barton-upon-Humber, UK, and former youth pastor

'Youth workers are very often not all-rounders! This book is a brilliant resource for someone like me—I always get stuck when it comes to planning games. For variety, simplicity and the fun factor, this book is what you need.'

—Sheila Stephen, lecturer in Youth & Children's Ministry, Wales Evangelical School of Theology

Also available

How to run children's clubs and meetings

Practical suggestions for
people in youth ministry

STEVEN WALKER

144PP, PAPERBACK

ISBN 978-1-84625-060-6

We would love to see people appear out of the blue who are superbly gifted at working with children and teenagers. These workers would have unlimited energy and patience, and be highly organized so that everything ran with barely a hitch.

Unfortunately, people like this are extremely rare. Perhaps you wonder whether you have what it takes to help with children's clubs. Maybe you already help with a children's club or meeting, but often feel that you are simply muddling along. You may have been helping with children's clubs for a number of years. Whatever your involvement in children's work, this Bible-based yet thoroughly practical book is designed to help you, as Steven Walker uses his considerable experience to provide encouragement as well as ideas and guidelines for all who assist with this ministry.

'...an attractive resource for all those who want to impact young lives to the glory of God.'

—J. Phil Arthur, Pastor, Free Grace Baptist Church, Lancaster, United Kingdom

ABOUT DAY ONE:

Day One's threefold commitment:

- To be faithful to the Bible, God's inerrant, infallible Word;
- To be relevant to our modern generation;
- To be excellent in our publication standards.

I continue to be thankful for the publications of Day One. They are biblical; they have sound theology; and they are relevant to the issues at hand. The material is condensed and manageable while, at the same time, being complete—a challenging balance to find. We are happy in our ministry to make use of these excellent publications.

JOHN MACARTHUR, PASTOR-TEACHER, GRACE COMMUNITY CHURCH, CALIFORNIA

It is a great encouragement to see Day One making such excellent progress. Their publications are always biblical, accessible and attractively produced, with no compromise on quality. Long may their progress continue and increase!

JOHN BLANCHARD, AUTHOR, EVANGELIST AND APOLOGIST

Visit our web site for more information and to request a free catalogue of our books.

www.dayone.co.uk

U.S. web site:

www.dayonebookstore.com